THIS JOURNAL BELONGS TO

PET *Profile*

NAME

NICK NAME

BIRTHDAY

ADOPTION DATE

PHOTO

· BASICS ·

WOOF!

BREED

GENDER

EYE COLOUR

COAT COLOUR

UNIQUE MARKINGS

SPAYED / NEUTERED

ID MICRO CHIP#

ALLERGIES

PERSONALITY TRAITS

FAVOURITE TOYS

FAVOURITE TREATS

🧰 MEDICINE *Tracker*

JANUARY	🐾	☐ WORMER
		☐ FLEA / TICK
FEBRUARY	🐾	☐ WORMER
		☐ FLEA / TICK

MARCH	🐾	☐ WORMER
		☐ FLEA / TICK
APRIL	🐾	☐ WORMER
		☐ FLEA / TICK

MAY	🐾	☐ WORMER
		☐ FLEA / TICK
JUNE	🐾	☐ WORMER
		☐ FLEA / TICK

JULY	🐾	☐ WORMER
		☐ FLEA / TICK
AUGUST	🐾	☐ WORMER
		☐ FLEA / TICK

SEPTEMBER	🐾	☐ WORMER
		☐ FLEA / TICK
OCTOBER	🐾	☐ WORMER
		☐ FLEA / TICK

NOVEMBER	🐾	☐ WORMER
		☐ FLEA / TICK
DECEMBER	🐾	☐ WORMER
		☐ FLEA / TICK

NOTES

PET *Vaccinations*

VET

ADDRESS

PHONE

E-MAIL

DATE	AGE	VACCINE	DUE DATE

GROWTH *Chart*

AGE	lbs	Oz
8 Weeks		
10 Weeks		
3 Months		
4 Months		
6 Months		
8 Months		
10 Months		
12 Months		

FIRST *Walk*

_____
_____
_____
_____
_____
_____
_____
_____

PHOTO

PET *Groomer*

NAME

ADDRESS

PHONE

E-MAIL

FIRST HAIR CUT

PHOTO

PAW Buddies

PHOTO

PHOTO

PHOTO

PHOTO

PET CARE *Chart*

WEEK COMMENCING _____

TIME	FOOD/WATER	ACCIDENT	WALK	TRAINING
MON				
TUE				
WED				
THUR				
FRI				
SAT				
SUN				

PROGRESS NOTES

PET CARE *Chart*

WEEK COMMENCING _____

	TIME	FOOD/WATER	ACCIDENT	WALK	TRAINING
MON					
TUE					
WED					
THUR					
FRI					
SAT					
SUN					

PROGRESS NOTES

PET CARE *Chart*

WEEK COMMENCING _____

	TIME	FOOD/WATER	ACCIDENT	WALK	TRAINING
MON					
TUE					
WED					
THUR					
FRI					
SAT					
SUN					

PROGRESS NOTES

PET CARE *Chart*

WEEK COMMENCING _____

	TIME	FOOD/WATER	ACCIDENT	WALK	TRAINING
MON					
TUE					
WED					
THUR					
FRI					
SAT					
SUN					

PROGRESS NOTES

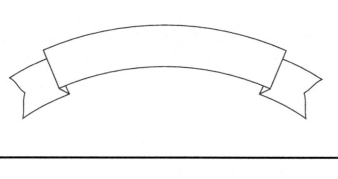

PET CARE *Chart*

WEEK COMMENCING _____

	TIME	FOOD/WATER	ACCIDENT	WALK	TRAINING
MON					
TUE					
WED					
THUR					
FRI					
SAT					
SUN					

PROGRESS NOTES

PET CARE *Chart*

WEEK COMMENCING _____

	TIME	FOOD/WATER	ACCIDENT	WALK	TRAINING
MON					
TUE					
WED					
THUR					
FRI					
SAT					
SUN					

PROGRESS NOTES

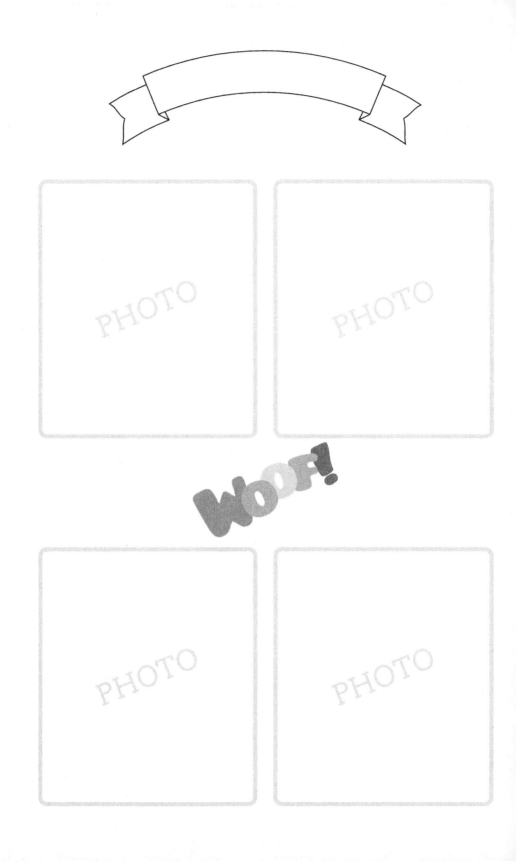

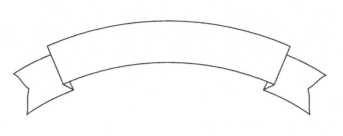

PET CARE *Chart*

WEEK COMMENCING _____

	TIME	FOOD/WATER	ACCIDENT	WALK	TRAINING
MON					
TUE					
WED					
THUR					
FRI					
SAT					
SUN					

PROGRESS NOTES

_____

_____

PET CARE *Chart*

WEEK COMMENCING _____

	TIME	FOOD/WATER	ACCIDENT	WALK	TRAINING
MON					
TUE					
WED					
THUR					
FRI					
SAT					
SUN					

PROGRESS NOTES

_____

_____

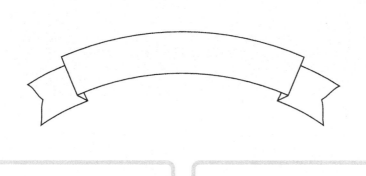

PET CARE *Chart*

WEEK COMMENCING _____

	TIME	FOOD/WATER	ACCIDENT	WALK	TRAINING
MON					
TUE					
WED					
THUR					
FRI					
SAT					
SUN					

PROGRESS NOTES

_____

_____

PET CARE *Chart*

WEEK COMMENCING _____

	TIME	FOOD/WATER	ACCIDENT	WALK	TRAINING
MON					
TUE					
WED					
THUR					
FRI					
SAT					
SUN					

PROGRESS NOTES

PET CARE *Chart*

WEEK COMMENCING _____

	TIME	FOOD/WATER	ACCIDENT	WALK	TRAINING
MON					
TUE					
WED					
THUR					
FRI					
SAT					
SUN					

PROGRESS NOTES

PET CARE *Chart*

WEEK COMMENCING _____

TIME	FOOD/WATER	ACCIDENT	WALK	TRAINING
MON				
TUE				
WED				
THUR				
FRI				
SAT				
SUN				

PROGRESS NOTES

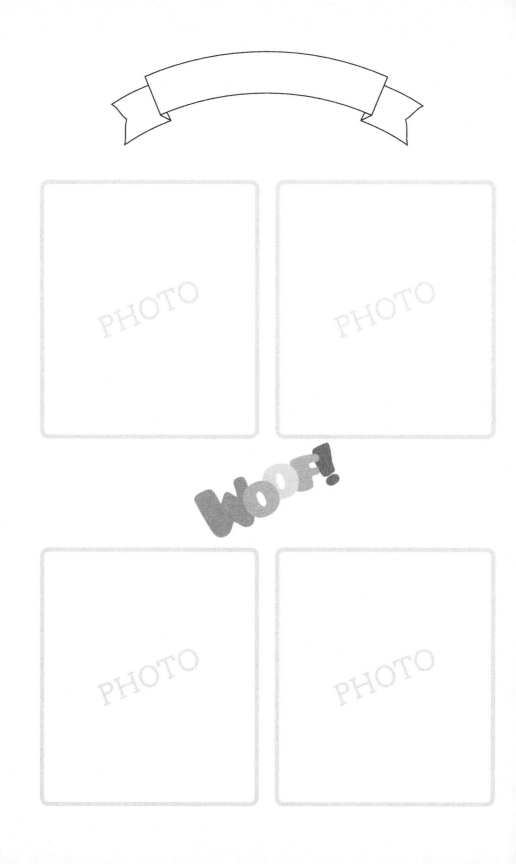

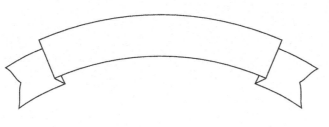

PET CARE *Chart*

WEEK COMMENCING _____

	TIME	FOOD/WATER	ACCIDENT	WALK	TRAINING
MON					
TUE					
WED					
THUR					
FRI					
SAT					
SUN					

PROGRESS NOTES

PET CARE *Chart*

	TIME	FOOD/WATER	ACCIDENT	WALK	TRAINING
MON					
TUE					
WED					
THUR					
FRI					
SAT					
SUN					

PROGRESS NOTES

PET CARE *Chart*

WEEK COMMENCING _____

	TIME	FOOD/WATER	ACCIDENT	WALK	TRAINING
MON					
TUE					
WED					
THUR					
FRI					
SAT					
SUN					

PROGRESS NOTES

PET CARE *Chart*

WEEK COMMENCING _____

	TIME	FOOD/WATER	ACCIDENT	WALK	TRAINING
MON					
TUE					
WED					
THUR					
FRI					
SAT					
SUN					

PROGRESS NOTES

PET CARE *Chart*

WEEK COMMENCING _____

	TIME	FOOD/WATER	ACCIDENT	WALK	TRAINING
MON					
TUE					
WED					
THUR					
FRI					
SAT					
SUN					

PROGRESS NOTES

PET CARE *Chart*

WEEK COMMENCING _____

	TIME	FOOD/WATER	ACCIDENT	WALK	TRAINING
MON					
TUE					
WED					
THUR					
FRI					
SAT					
SUN					

PROGRESS NOTES

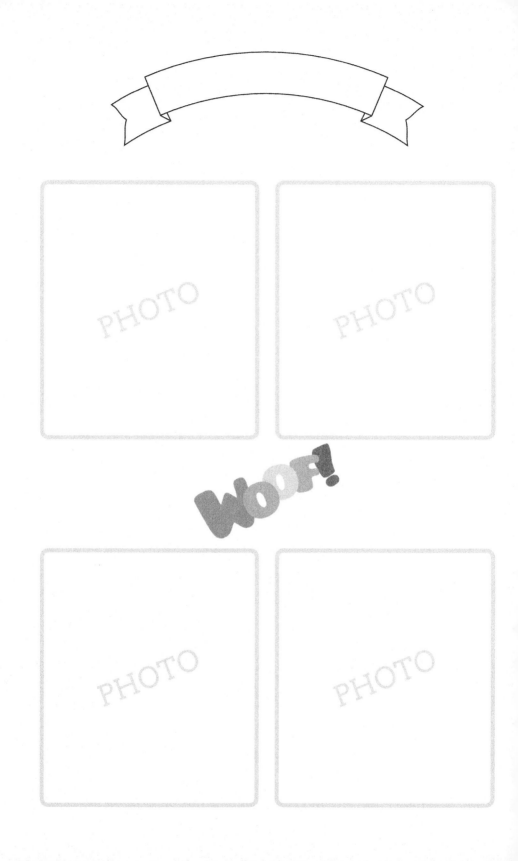

PET CARE *Chart*

WEEK COMMENCING _____

	TIME	FOOD/WATER	ACCIDENT	WALK	TRAINING
MON					
TUE					
WED					
THUR					
FRI					
SAT					
SUN					

PROGRESS NOTES

PET CARE *Chart*

WEEK COMMENCING _____

	TIME	FOOD/WATER	ACCIDENT	WALK	TRAINING
MON					
TUE					
WED					
THUR					
FRI					
SAT					
SUN					

PROGRESS NOTES

PET CARE *Chart*

WEEK COMMENCING _____

	TIME	FOOD/WATER	ACCIDENT	WALK	TRAINING
MON					
TUE					
WED					
THUR					
FRI					
SAT					
SUN					

PROGRESS NOTES

_____

_____

PET CARE *Chart*

WEEK COMMENCING _____

	TIME	FOOD/WATER	ACCIDENT	WALK	TRAINING
MON					
TUE					
WED					
THUR					
FRI					
SAT					
SUN					

PROGRESS NOTES

_____

_____

PET CARE *Chart*

WEEK COMMENCING _____

	TIME	FOOD/WATER	ACCIDENT	WALK	TRAINING
MON					
TUE					
WED					
THUR					
FRI					
SAT					
SUN					

PROGRESS NOTES

_____

_____

PET CARE *Chart*

WEEK COMMENCING _____

	TIME	FOOD/WATER	ACCIDENT	WALK	TRAINING
MON					
TUE					
WED					
THUR					
FRI					
SAT					
SUN					

PROGRESS NOTES

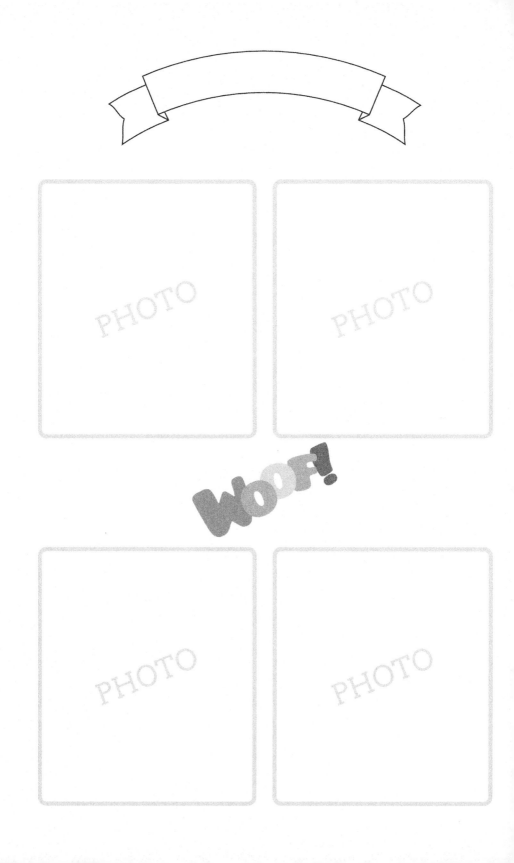

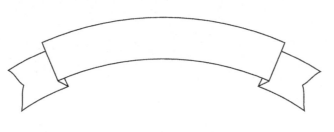

PET CARE *Chart*

WEEK COMMENCING _____

	TIME	FOOD/WATER	ACCIDENT	WALK	TRAINING
MON					
TUE					
WED					
THUR					
FRI					
SAT					
SUN					

PROGRESS NOTES

PET CARE *Chart*

WEEK COMMENCING _____

	TIME	FOOD/WATER	ACCIDENT	WALK	TRAINING
MON					
TUE					
WED					
THUR					
FRI					
SAT					
SUN					

PROGRESS NOTES

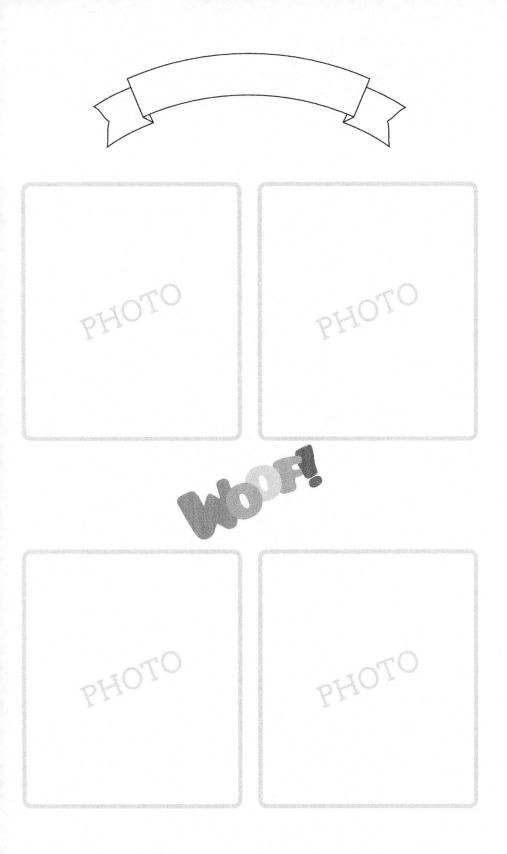

PET CARE *Chart*

WEEK COMMENCING _____

TIME	FOOD/WATER	ACCIDENT	WALK	TRAINING
MON				
TUE				
WED				
THUR				
FRI				
SAT				
SUN				

PROGRESS NOTES

_____

_____

PET CARE *Chart*

WEEK COMMENCING _____

	TIME	FOOD/WATER	ACCIDENT	WALK	TRAINING
MON					
TUE					
WED					
THUR					
FRI					
SAT					
SUN					

PROGRESS NOTES

_____

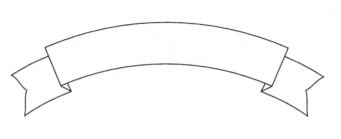

PET CARE *Chart*

WEEK COMMENCING _____

	TIME	FOOD/WATER	ACCIDENT	WALK	TRAINING
MON					
TUE					
WED					
THUR					
FRI					
SAT					
SUN					

PROGRESS NOTES

PET CARE *Chart*

WEEK COMMENCING _____

TIME	FOOD/WATER	ACCIDENT	WALK	TRAINING
MON				
TUE				
WED				
THUR				
FRI				
SAT				
SUN				

PROGRESS NOTES

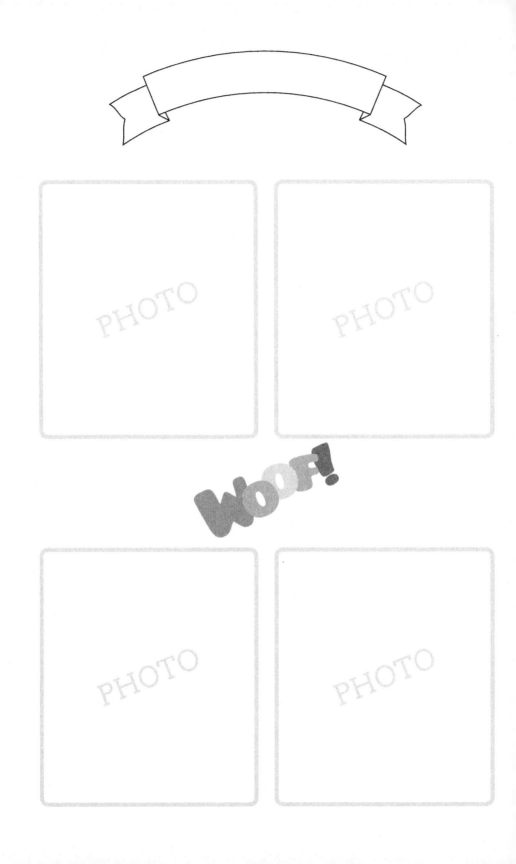

PET CARE *Chart*

WEEK COMMENCING _____

	TIME	FOOD/WATER	ACCIDENT	WALK	TRAINING
MON					
TUE					
WED					
THUR					
FRI					
SAT					
SUN					

PROGRESS NOTES

PET CARE *Chart*

WEEK COMMENCING _____

	TIME	FOOD/WATER	ACCIDENT	WALK	TRAINING
MON					
TUE					
WED					
THUR					
FRI					
SAT					
SUN					

PROGRESS NOTES

_____

_____

PET CARE *Chart*

WEEK COMMENCING _____

	TIME	FOOD/WATER	ACCIDENT	WALK	TRAINING
MON					
TUE					
WED					
THUR					
FRI					
SAT					
SUN					

PROGRESS NOTES

PET CARE *Chart*

WEEK COMMENCING _____

TIME	FOOD/WATER	ACCIDENT	WALK	TRAINING
MON				
TUE				
WED				
THUR				
FRI				
SAT				
SUN				

PROGRESS NOTES

_____

_____

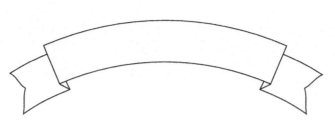

PET CARE *Chart*

WEEK COMMENCING _____

	TIME	FOOD/WATER	ACCIDENT	WALK	TRAINING
MON					
TUE					
WED					
THUR					
FRI					
SAT					
SUN					

PROGRESS NOTES

_____

_____

PET CARE *Chart*

WEEK COMMENCING _____

TIME	FOOD/WATER	ACCIDENT	WALK	TRAINING
MON				
TUE				
WED				
THUR				
FRI				
SAT				
SUN				

PROGRESS NOTES

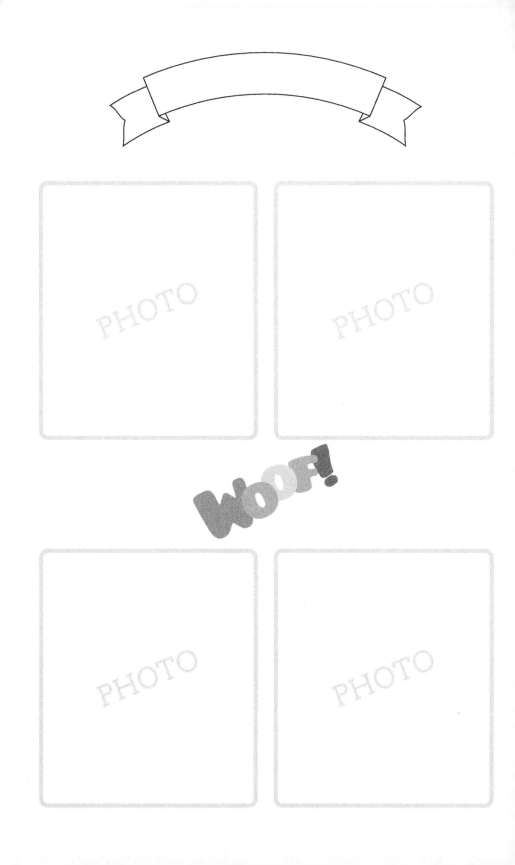

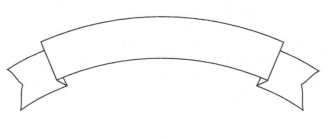

PET CARE *Chart*

WEEK COMMENCING _____

	TIME	FOOD/WATER	ACCIDENT	WALK	TRAINING
MON					
TUE					
WED					
THUR					
FRI					
SAT					
SUN					

PROGRESS NOTES

_____

_____

PET CARE *Chart*

WEEK COMMENCING _____

	TIME	FOOD/WATER	ACCIDENT	WALK	TRAINING
MON					
TUE					
WED					
THUR					
FRI					
SAT					
SUN					

PROGRESS NOTES

_____

_____

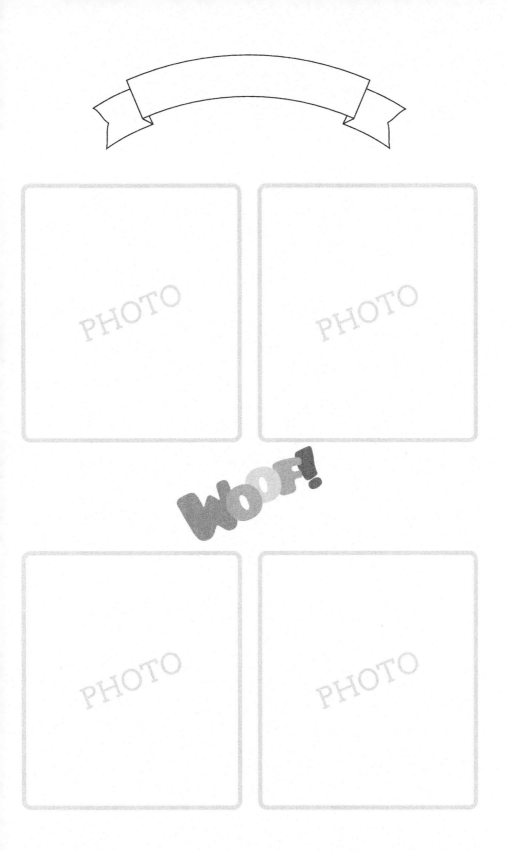

PET CARE *Chart*

WEEK COMMENCING _____

	TIME	FOOD/WATER	ACCIDENT	WALK	TRAINING
MON					
TUE					
WED					
THUR					
FRI					
SAT					
SUN					

PROGRESS NOTES

PET CARE *Chart*

WEEK COMMENCING _____

	TIME	FOOD/WATER	ACCIDENT	WALK	TRAINING
MON					
TUE					
WED					
THUR					
FRI					
SAT					
SUN					

PROGRESS NOTES

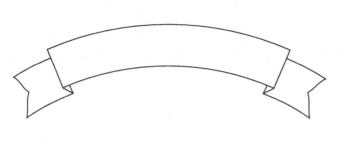

PET CARE *Chart*

WEEK COMMENCING _____

	TIME	FOOD/WATER	ACCIDENT	WALK	TRAINING
MON					
TUE					
WED					
THUR					
FRI					
SAT					
SUN					

PROGRESS NOTES

PET CARE *Chart*

WEEK COMMENCING _____

	TIME	FOOD/WATER	ACCIDENT	WALK	TRAINING
MON					
TUE					
WED					
THUR					
FRI					
SAT					
SUN					

PROGRESS NOTES

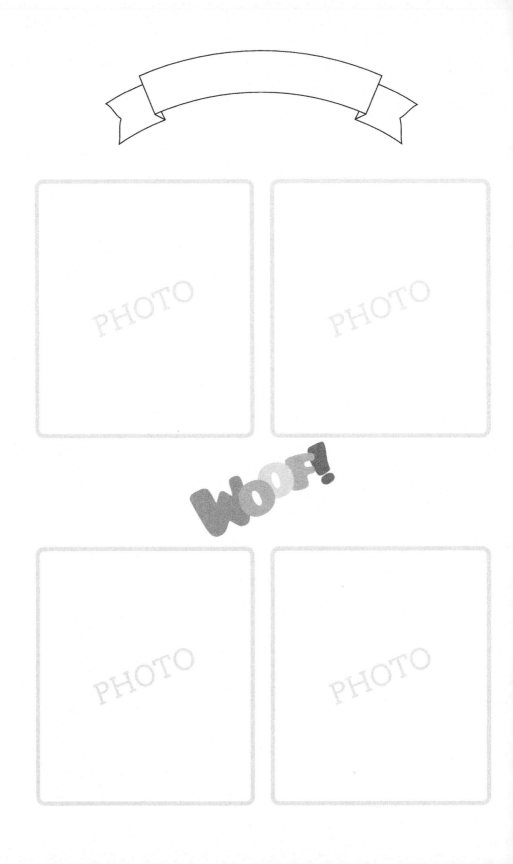

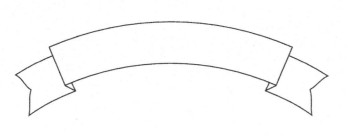

PET CARE *Chart*

WEEK COMMENCING _____

	TIME	FOOD/WATER	ACCIDENT	WALK	TRAINING
MON					
TUE					
WED					
THUR					
FRI					
SAT					
SUN					

PROGRESS NOTES

_____

_____

PET CARE *Chart*

WEEK COMMENCING _____

	TIME	FOOD/WATER	ACCIDENT	WALK	TRAINING
MON					
TUE					
WED					
THUR					
FRI					
SAT					
SUN					

PROGRESS NOTES

_____

_____

PET CARE *Chart*

WEEK COMMENCING _____

	TIME	FOOD/WATER	ACCIDENT	WALK	TRAINING
MON					
TUE					
WED					
THUR					
FRI					
SAT					
SUN					

PROGRESS NOTES

_____

_____

PET CARE *Chart*

WEEK COMMENCING _____

	TIME	FOOD/WATER	ACCIDENT	WALK	TRAINING
MON					
TUE					
WED					
THUR					
FRI					
SAT					
SUN					

PROGRESS NOTES

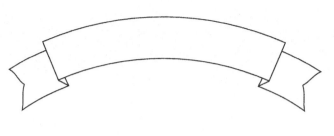

PET CARE *Chart*

WEEK COMMENCING _____

	TIME	FOOD/WATER	ACCIDENT	WALK	TRAINING
MON					
TUE					
WED					
THUR					
FRI					
SAT					
SUN					

PROGRESS NOTES

_____

_____

PET CARE *Chart*

WEEK COMMENCING _____

	TIME	FOOD/WATER	ACCIDENT	WALK	TRAINING
MON					
TUE					
WED					
THUR					
FRI					
SAT					
SUN					

PROGRESS NOTES

_____

_____

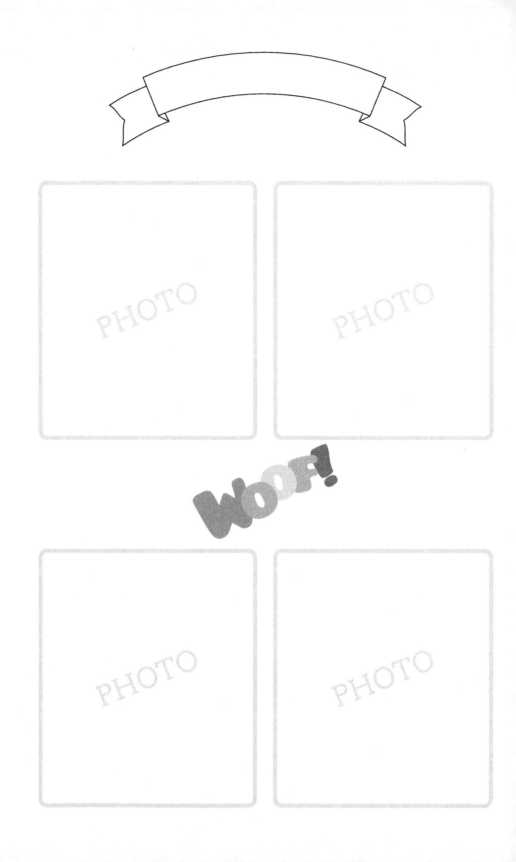

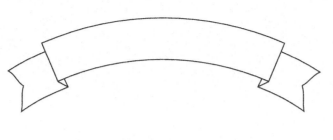

PET CARE *Chart*

WEEK COMMENCING _____

	TIME	FOOD/WATER	ACCIDENT	WALK	TRAINING
MON					
TUE					
WED					
THUR					
FRI					
SAT					
SUN					

PROGRESS NOTES

PET CARE *Chart*

	TIME	FOOD/WATER	ACCIDENT	WALK	TRAINING
MON					
TUE					
WED					
THUR					
FRI					
SAT					
SUN					

PROGRESS NOTES

PET CARE *Chart*

WEEK COMMENCING _____

	TIME	FOOD/WATER	ACCIDENT	WALK	TRAINING
MON					
TUE					
WED					
THUR					
FRI					
SAT					
SUN					

PROGRESS NOTES

_____

_____

PET CARE *Chart*

WEEK COMMENCING _____

	TIME	FOOD/WATER	ACCIDENT	WALK	TRAINING
MON					
TUE					
WED					
THUR					
FRI					
SAT					
SUN					

PROGRESS NOTES

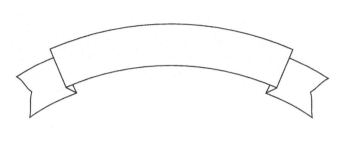

PET CARE *Chart*

WEEK COMMENCING _____

	TIME	FOOD/WATER	ACCIDENT	WALK	TRAINING
MON					
TUE					
WED					
THUR					
FRI					
SAT					
SUN					

PROGRESS NOTES

PET CARE *Chart*

WEEK COMMENCING _____

	TIME	FOOD/WATER	ACCIDENT	WALK	TRAINING
MON					
TUE					
WED					
THUR					
FRI					
SAT					
SUN					

PROGRESS NOTES

_____

_____

1 TODAY

PHOTO

HOW WE CELEBRATED

Printed in Great Britain
by Amazon

73001101R00072